CREATIVE DEVELOPMENT

CREATIVE
DEVELOPMENT

Five Lectures to
Art Students

REG BUTLER

Routledge and Kegan Paul
LONDON

First published 1962
by Routledge and Kegan Paul Ltd
Broadway House, 68–74 Carter Lane
London, E.C.4

Printed in Great Britain
by Western Printing Services Ltd, Bristol

Contents

These lectures were given at the Slade School, University College, London, in June 1961.

One: The 'Laws' of Development

TRADITIONALLY, the artist is expected to talk about art; to say a few words about a plastic object in front of him, or to make a few tentative suggestions about what he regards as his own objectives. Very frequently the artist will talk at length about the impossibility of discussing anything.

I wish, however, to consider matters which are by their nature discussable, in other words, ideas: ideas connected with painting and sculpture, but more overtly with the problem of the development of the artist. I prefer to talk about creative development, even though it may sound a little pompous, because I want to avoid the semantic attachments connected with the idea of art education. Education suggests too passive a position on the part of the student; it suggests an educational body which educates and a student who receives education. Obviously all adult teaching is a form of brainwashing, but there is no need to pride oneself on the fact. It is a matter of indifference to me whether a student orders the pattern of his own artistic growth or whether for a period of time he puts himself in the hands of a body ostensibly devoted to that end. I am quite convinced that in general art schools do not produce better artists, they only produce a different kind of artist, and the subjects I propose we discuss are as relevant to a young man setting out to discover whether or not he has talent, while working in an office or in a factory, as to a pampered and oversupported student working in an organization dedicated wholly to his welfare.

This afternoon I propose we consider a very wide field, one which unavoidably involves considerable generalization: I offer for consideration two propositions which, in the manner of Mr Parkinson, I shall call Butler's laws of creative development:

(1) All other things being equal,
    development is proportional to exposure.
(2) Development is proportional to motivation,
    which is inversely proportional to adjustment.

The objective of every art student worth the name should be that of becoming a great artist; I do not boggle at the term, and I do not consider that any lesser ambition is worth consideration here. Those of you who look forward to becoming art teachers or hope to enrich your lives between now and marriage do not, in my opinion, deserve the sort of support I have in mind. If you do not feel in your bones that you have it in you to become great creative artists, I suggest you would be better employed in training yourselves to make money in any of the thousand and one occupations dedicated to that objective.

To elaborate law one:

    development is proportional to exposure.

Being possessed of a healthy and vigorous creative urge, the student's horizon will widen, his understanding of the problems of previous generations of artists, and his opportunities to bissociate constructively (bissociation in my opinion is a good definition of creativity) will be proportional to the variety, the richness, and the general intensity of the experiences to which he is exposed. The exposure of students to a wide range of artistic experience should be the first thought of those planning a curriculum. But not only should the spectrum of experience be wide; the sequence of experience is also of very great importance.

The first preoccupation of the young art student, and one which might well begin long before his entry into an art school, should be to acquaint himself with the origins of the character of the world in which he lives, and in which his initial period of activity will take place. He should therefore, to begin with, be provided with opportunities of studying the art of the past, including the art of this morning as well as of yesterday. He would be well advised to acquaint himself with what appears to be known of the relationship between the kind of work artists have done, and the character of the social and technical climate in which they lived. He will see, for instance, that carving stone was not in fact an arbitrary activity for an inhabitant of ancient Egypt, but the inevitable corollary of the situation in which the Egyptian artist found himself. He will realize that the art of drawing in general followed the invention of paper, and that the eclecticism of the twentieth century is a characteristic of what may well be a social malaise. He will thereby realize, I hope, that he cannot be taught 'the forms of art' as though they were immutable canons, for he will understand that historical processes are at work every single second, shaping the future, and that these same processes will ultimately determine the precise forms of his work. I hope he will come to realize that in art 'received pronunciation' is sterile, inexpressive, a negation of life itself, a mere contemporary shibboleth. This should help him to decide at an early stage in his life that he will do well to examine with deep and constant suspicion any systems of thought or action which may be offered him.

During this period he should, I suggest, acquaint himself, as efficiently as possible, with the technical means available for making paintings, sculptures, lithographs, and so on. If, for instance, he is suited by nature to become a sculptor, he will find no difficulty in learning to weld with oxyacetylene or the electric arc in a fortnight; to cast in bronze by the *cire perdue* method, or to make sand castings, in an equal period. He will rapidly acquaint himself with the techniques of plaster moulding, the use of synthetic moulding materials, etc., and realize that all the teaching he may be given on the subject of stone carving can be compressed into one day. This is not to say that he will become, in a matter of months, proficient in these

4

technical undertakings, but he will realize that all that stands between him and the proficiency of a Cellini or a Bernini will be a period spent in practice. For a student suited by nature to be a sculptor there are in my opinion no technical difficulties worth the name. Skill is the least requirement, because it is the one that can be acquired.

I see many practical advantages in the study of history and the development of technical ability taking place simultaneously. The intellectual strain of historical study is advantageously offset by the pleasurable aspect of manual labour. To spend one's day carving stone, or setting up an armature to carry a mass of clay, or attacking a tree trunk with an adze, and the evening reading the works of Cellini, Professor Gombrich, or Sir Herbert Read, is an invigorating pattern of life, and one for which a student should find immense resources of energy.

Having informed himself on the nature of and speculated on some of the causes of the forms of the art of the past, and acquainted himself with the main characteristics of the facilities at present available for making art-objects, the second stage of exposure should occur. I must describe this second stage as the development of traditional artistic abilities. This is not a very good label, because it is based on the widespread fallacy that traditional art is the art of the Renaissance. However, it is a handy enough term provided you remember that by it I mean acquiring the skill of drawing or modelling a hand which has five fingers, and is made of bone and muscle and flesh and skin, so that an independent observer examining the result of your labours will conclude that your document refers to a hand which has five fingers and is made of bone and muscle and flesh and skin. In other words, making a statement from life in such a way that it roughly corresponds with the experience of most of us.

Little if any justification is needed, I imagine, to persuade you that you should give some consideration to the history of art, the character of the world in which you live, and the technical apparatus available today; you may, however, feel that to advocate the traditional art school grind needs considerable support. To be frank, I have little sympathy with those who would attempt to justify life-class study on the basis of a moral assertion that you ought to do it because it is the only way to develop your abilities as an artist—what I call the artmanship argument.

Skill in objective drawing and modelling is by no means the essential key to expressive creative work. There have been so-called naïve artists, who without employing any such skills have made profoundly moving statements of great artistic merit. It may well be that a period of a man's life spent in such modelling or drawing will do nothing more than make him a different kind of artist from what he would have been without it. I am certainly not going to insist that this is the only way, but neither am I, nor I think should anyone else, be prepared to say 'I know that it is unnecessary'. The whole problem of art education must

6

be approached on the basis that we do not know what we can afford to leave out. We do not know what is the ideal pattern of exposure in order to encourage the greatest development of a student's talent. We do not, in fact, know enough to exclude this.

Still on the subject of exposure—if, for the sake of argument, two years have been spent in a study of history and the technical aspects of making art, and two further years in acquiring some degree of traditional artistic experience, then I think at least an equal period should be spent in what I would call supported freedom. In practical terms this would mean the financial support of a student, including the provision of a private place in which to work and of models if he so desired, the provision of a body of tutors available to assist him —again only if he so desired, and an ambience of people engaged in similar activities, though not sharing his actual working premises. I mean that affairs should be so contrived that for these last two years the student should work freely on activities entirely of his own choice, uninterrupted by financial worries, or the attention of overzealous tutors; free from the oppressive burden of any external *a priori* criteria such as a diploma, and yet having at his beck and call all the contacts and technical assistance he might want. During this period he would, in my opinion, consider himself exposed to the problem of getting along with himself as an artist—following his nose to see where it might lead him, sympathetic to the vitality and inspiration of his own creative accidents, free to try and fail in a thousand and one crazy experiments without fear of criticism, loss of face, or danger of losing support.

A wise student should always make the greatest effort to find himself somewhere to work entirely alone, and a wise educational body should do everything possible to find accommodation for private studios. I have often thought it wrong to expect a high level of creative work from art students sharing a common studio. The kind of experiments which pay off are seriously inhibited by the presence of other students, and I would gladly reduce the number of art students in this country by 90 per cent if it meant that the remaining 10 per cent could spend their last two years of State support working in privacy except when they chose otherwise. Again, a period of genuine creative freedom is the only way a student can reveal his artistic as opposed to his scholastic ability, and thus enable trusts, foundations, and scholarship bodies to make a wise selection.

And now to the second law:

Development is proportional to motivation
which is inversely proportional to adjustment.

In one respect at least creative artists are the same as everyone else; their motivational drives are the same: self-preservation, sex, and power. Equally, exceptional artists—like exceptional men in general—are powerfully motivated individuals. No matter how well-planned the environment of an art student, either by himself or by an educational institution, his artistic growth will be pallid, formless, and without vigour if he lacks the irrational urge, the drive, which will make him feel that every moment spent in drawing or painting, carving or modelling, is a moment well spent—an end in itself and not a means to something else. Not a means to getting a diploma, not a means to getting a teaching job, and not a means to possessing a Series E Jaguar.

This is not the place to go deeply into the theories of Jung or Freud or the persuasions of behaviourists as to the origins of creative drive in the human animal, but notwithstanding the essential normality of play in the human child, it seems to me, from such thought as I have been able to give to the question, that the urgency of creative desire springs from those individuals who for one reason or another are out of balance with their environment. For the creation of a vital work of art involves a release of emotional tension, and where no such tensions exist the roots of art do not exist either.

It is not, I think, unduly far-fetched to describe the creative human animal as a creature with an over-developed emotional cortex, and even if you regard the artist as a simple case of arrested adolescence, this may equally be described as an abnormality—provided, of course, that you place no great store by the quality of being normal. An artist's desire to replace fact by fantasy, his divine discontent, his desire to create an orderly or coherent pattern where none exists, or even his compulsive necessity merely to formulate a process —all these can be seen as attempts to reorganize certain aspects of his environment. In contrast you have the contented animal who seeks little if anything beyond food, rest, and from time to time sex.

Now, whether an artist's drive springs from a lack of psycho-sexual balance, suppressed sadism, a need to confront himself with the evidence that women are different from men, or whatever, I think it is obvious that these drives are at their height shortly after adoles-cence, and that in many human beings such states of abnormality become resolved by middle age. This fact is in my opinion the only indisputable justification for organized art education. Development must not be delayed.

Of course, in different men the peak of creative ability occurs at somewhat different ages, but I would hazard a guess that it is probably at its greatest where the individual acquires skill at a sufficiently early age for this to coincide with a sustained emotional drive. However much skill and experience an artist may develop in later life, it cannot result in great work if, so to say, he has by that time settled down, discovered a measure of contentment, and philosophically adapted himself to the realities.

In art, as in other occupations, many are called but few are chosen, and the motivation of a student may be satisfied by the acquisition of a diploma, or the esteem of his tutors and the admiration of his fellows. After that what is there for him to do but to continue to make such professional use as he may of the skills he has acquired? Another, by constant attendance at the life class, by becoming as it were a licensed voyeur, may well reach a relaxed and relatively tranquil acceptance of the facts of life through this constant opportunity of viewing the opposite sex, at leisure and in detail.

Again I am quite sure the vitality of a great many female students derives from frustrated maternity, and most of these, on finding the opportunity to settle down and produce children, will no longer experience a degree of passionate discontent sufficient to drive them constantly towards the labours of creation in other ways. There are biological differences between men and women which it has become fashionable to ignore; the high proportion of female art students is a consequence of this.

For the frustrated voyeur there is little that the art school can do short of forbidding him to have more than an occasional peep through the door of the life room, and the case of frustrated maternity is largely beyond the jurisdiction of the tutors. There is in fact only one respect in which the art school can avoid actively dissipating creative drive, and this is in connection with diplomas, prizes, and awards for good behaviour generally.

From time to time one is told that so and so might have been a great artist had he not been to such and such an art school, which, it is alleged, destroyed his talent! My reply is always, 'Then he must have had very little talent to begin with.' It is true, of course, that an art school is a risky place in many ways, but I do not think we should waste our tears on those whose needs to create have been satisfied by maternity, by diplomas, or by positions of responsibility.

But the diploma does present an avoidable risk. It may so very readily become a moral objective, a kind of *good*, substituting its own values for those of art, and in this respect may have a considerable delaying effect upon an otherwise creative student. There are not, I hope, many tutors who set great store by the diploma as such. I am sure diplomas are very largely created to comfort Treasury departments, local authorities, and the whole world of those who fear that public money may be misspent—may find its way to irresponsible young people who will use it merely to have a good time! We ought to prefer to see a million pounds of public money thus misspent than one potentially creative student hag-ridden by a false shibboleth.

It should be the constant duty of the tutor to persuade the student that what he must seek beyond all else is his own approval, this of course being in the certainty that where a truly creative nature is concerned it is the last thing he is likely to find. The task of assuring students that their objective should not be the approval of the hierarchy which surrounds them is important, but is one too frequently overlooked.

If I suggest that there is little the art school can do to prevent a decay of motivation in the case of the majority of students, there are at least a number of positive things which, in favourable circumstances, will promote or increase creative drive.

The proper teaching of history, so that social as well as personal objectives become possible. This is a difficult question today, and one which I hope we shall discuss in detail in later lectures.

The ruthless exclusion from art schools of all doubtful candidates, so that the tempo and vitality of a student's contemporaries is maximized.

The provision of an exciting and ever-changing series of display photographs is important, also of loaned works of art, of scientific information, in fact a constantly unfolding *musée imaginaire*. This is bound to be of enormous value, for none can say what will or will not be a catalyst, a trigger for any particular student.

On the whole I think very little harm comes from bad tutors; the only people they are likely to influence would perhaps be bad artists anyway. Nevertheless bad tutors do mean delayed development, and the problem of staffing the contemporary art school becomes increasingly difficult every year.

It was, I think, Paul Klee who said, 'No good artist should teach, and no one should teach who is not a good artist'—a pretty exclusive doctrine, but there is, I think, a very great deal in it. For notwithstanding the occurrence here and there of dedicated men and women with a real vocation for teaching, there are two

factors peculiar to this century which make the situation unimaginably difficult.

The first factor is due to the victory of modern art.
Up to the thirties the majority of art schools in Europe
generally, not in this country only, were staffed by
so-called academic tutors (I say so-called because had
they been truly academic they could not have avoided a
degree of enlightenment which they obviously did not
possess), and these gentleman were concerned—not
only in painting and sculpture but in architecture and
music—in a fierce rearguard action to maintain a *status
quo* belonging properly speaking to the beginning of
the nineteenth century. Bad as these people were, their
group dynamic at least provided a barrier to be over-
come, and the students in those days derived enormous
stimulus from this situation. The people at the top were
so obviously pigheaded, so obviously unprincipled, so
unquestionably determined to hold back all liberating
ideas, that everyone had the greatest satisfaction in
joining battle, the greatest sense of achievement at every
small victory. But today the old guard is so manifestly
routed, so obviously discredited, that even those who
secretly subscribe to its precepts lack the nerve to stand
up for their beliefs.

The tutors of today are too ready to lean over backwards in order to avoid being thought unsympathetic,
narrow-minded, and this leaves the student body with
too little opposition. A vital opposition is a necessary
thing, both to the individual and to the group, but this

opposition must occur in exactly the right degree if it is to be fully beneficial—it must be in fact an optimum. Too much opposition, and the individual is swamped and obliterated; too little, and his energies find nothing with which to come to grips. I see few signs at the moment of the situation improving, and this, I think, is partly due to a second factor which is peculiar to the present time; I mean the extent to which the bour-geoisie is inclined to embrace the artist, to reward him with a living which is such that only those with a deep sense of social responsibility are disposed to give the time necessary to making contact with students. Thirty years ago even the most brilliant creative painters and sculptors found it none too easy to earn a living, and there was at least a financial incentive which encouraged them to accept teaching positions. But today there are perhaps no creative artists of proved creative vitality who need, in any financial sense of the word, to contri-bute to their living by teaching, and the art schools of the world will, I think, at least in the foreseeable future, have to rely more and more on second-rate talent.

In my own life nothing has been more stimulating than contact with truly creative people, and providing you do not expect your great creative artist to be any-thing other than a thoroughly human individual I do not imagine that you will be disappointed either. But five minutes with a Giacometti is not only worth more than five years with a clinical case of the art-hating—nature-loving syndrome, but it is also more practical than a great many principals seem inclined to think. The vital, interested, active student has a great deal to contribute from his own resources, and I think it should be the responsibility of every decent art school to do all it can to entice the visiting artist, even for extremely brief visits.

The use of the tape recorder as a means of distributing views and conversations could be developed much more than it has been up to the moment, and I am sure many more artists of international worth would be found prepared to contribute to the teaching picture were they approached in the right way and not expected to experience the unbelievable boredom which a visit to a school so often involves.

I have said that motivation is inversely proportional to adjustment. In life generally the rule is adjust and carry on, but in art to adjust means to die, and it is the responsibility of all teaching bodies to ensure that the flexibility and evolutionary vitality of their organization shall be such that adjustment on the part of their students is a practical impossibility. Once work in a school becomes a matter of routine, that school has failed in its primary function, and governing bodies have a responsibility to maintain a constant state of flux. It is criminal if the only thing new about an art school can be said to be its students.

You will gather that I favour a serial form of development rather than a parallel one; that is to say, a scheme whereby history and technology are followed by traditional art school teaching, and this is then followed by a definite period of creative freedom. I am aware that this may sound a rather old fashioned suggestion—the emphasis in very many art schools today (which pride themselves on an *avant garde* attitude) appears to be based on the idea that mixing technology with studio practice, and creative freedom with history, and so on, maintains the student's interest. This it may well do to some extent, but I feel it has grave disadvantages. It very readily induces a kind of intellectual emotional confusion whereby the student hardly knows whether he is creating a work of art or whether he is engaged on some preparatory exercise to fit him for his future creative work later in life. Study becomes confused with creative release, technology is skimped because the student's mind is adjusted to other importances, and the conscientious student may on the one hand be diverted from the development of a habit of slow continuous creative concentration so that he may give attention to technical or historical lectures, or on the other hand his interest in a sudden realization of historical significance may divert him from his studio work.

I do not wish to pursue this point in further detail at this stage—for one thing I am sure many of you already hold strong views for or against this suggestion, and I do not wish to anticipate your criticisms. I would like to say, however, that in my opinion this amorphous pattern stems from a contemporary confusion of ideas, the woolly headed argument going something like this! The true character and function of the twentieth-century artist is an anarchic one, he works in a free ambience expressing himself according to the dictates of his own persuasions. He is continually introducing new definitions of value. The present state of art, in other words, is amorphous, therefore we must expect the shape of our art education to be amorphous as well.

This is putting the highest possible interpretation on the attitude. At a lower level it could be argued that the muddled structure of present-day art education is due to a lack of conviction on the part of educators in general—a fear that a too regimented pattern might destroy creative sensibility. Art must be pre-orgasmic—so should art education!—but this need not be synonymous with confusion and chaos.

The last question I want you to consider is in some ways the most difficult one for me to raise here.

To obtain a lively and stimulating atmosphere a much more ruthless attitude towards weaker students is absolutely essential. Too many would-be painters and sculptors are given the benefit of the doubt, and it is far too easy to get support for four years at an art school. The butter on the bread in fact is spread far too thin, and the really promising student lacks financial support and facilities in consequence.

Whenever I mention this I am told, 'How can you assess a man's potential ability, how can you avoid making grave mistakes?' There is something to be said for this attitude, nevertheless I think it is a false one. Enormous progress has been made in the last ten years in the matter of candidate selection in general, and I see no reason why some of the knowledge gained in other fields should not be applied in the arts. Obviously mistakes will be made; talent is not easily assessible, and will be overlooked, but this will not, in my opinion, deprive the world of a single potentially great artist. For one thing I am quite convinced that formal training is by no means essential, and genius has an invariable way of finding its route to the top. Were unlimited finances available I would not press this point, but this is not the case, and it is morally wrong not to maintain the most efficient sifting and sorting mechanism we can devise. For it is a wicked thing to encourage an untalented student to spend four years of his life pursuing an interest in which he stands very little chance of gaining much success. One should not forget that on the whole a student is less fitted to earn his living after four years than before he commences.

Separating the men from the boys at the beginning and during the early stages of any course should be handled much more ruthlessly. Spending one's life making paintings or sculptures is not a normal human activity, and being a painter or a sculptor is not the same as being a professional man. Regarding yourself as a qualified sculptor today is as ridiculous as claiming to be a qualified poet.

Huxley's *Brave New World* is coming into being

much more quickly than either he or anyone else imagined, and in that world—whether we like it or not—the creative artist is an outsider. In fifty years from now it may well be that any young man who expresses a desire to be a painter or a sculptor will be gently led to a psychiatrist's waiting-room and told that he will receive treatment and doubtless recover in due course. We are not in that situation yet, nevertheless even today indiscriminate encouragement is in my opinion morally and socially wrong.

Among the questions which I feel need wide discussion I would include the following:

1. Can an art school reasonably hope to provide satisfactorily for possible creative genius and more pedestrian talent? Are not these utterly different objectives?

2. To what extent do you think that historical determinism invalidates the whole idea of teaching art?

3. Do you think technology can profitably be studied initially isolated from normal creative activity?

4. Do you justify the traditional life-class grind? If so how? Do you justify eliminating the traditional life-class grind? If so how?

5. Group study is certainly possible, but does anyone not think that creativity is hampered by lack of privacy?

6. Would you think it worthwhile to provide

private studios for last-stage students even if it meant considerably reducing the number of students in art schools in this country?

7. Is there any definition under which an artist may be regarded as a normal animal?

8. Can a woman become a vital creative artist without ceasing to be a woman except for purposes of census?

9. Do you agree that *vis-à-vis* art a diploma is a false incentive—a professional device appropriate to architecture and medicine but positively a dangerous surrogate in an art school?

10. Do you think emotional opposition is vitally necessary? If so, how could it best be provided?

11. What rewards other than financial do you think an art school can offer a practising artist to secure his attentions?

12. What is the case against parallel as against serial development?

13. Do you not consider that it is too easy to become an art student today?

Two: History

BECAUSE every human enterprise is framed by its historical context, our past is not only our springboard but it is also our straitjacket—together with the whole of nature, we are part of an evolving process, and the character of this process is not in my view incomprehensible, but it is one for which our present models are far from adequate.

Some of you may be convinced determinists, others may hold equally strongly to a belief in free will. I believe both attitudes as accurate models leave much to be desired, and that the generally accepted concepts of free will and determinism are by no means incompatible, except in so far that they operate at different levels.

Now, just as the forms of nature are a consequence of long evolutionary processes, so, in my opinion, are the forms of art, and the conditions which gave rise to a painting by Michelangelo need not, I think, in essence, be different from those which have resulted in the configuration of the English coastline.

You do what you do because you are who you are,

and I am what I am because of whence I am come. Everything we do is a consequence of our personal history within the history of our species. The forms of my sculpture and your painting are a function of our biological and cultural evolution. Their origins may be mysterious, but they are not it seems to me mystical.

This afternoon we discuss the place of history in creative development; the contribution it may make to the artist's evolution as an artist and the dangers he may run from the awareness it may generate in him.

There are advantages in putting the question in the crudest possible terms. Can a wide appreciation of history help you to make better art? I believe it can. Certainly for those of you capable of greatness it will give you your only chance of becoming great artists—as opposed to merely good artists. For great art differs from good art by virtue of its range as well as its intensity, and this question is one of special interest just at this time. There is little doubt in my mind that the art of the immediate past is that of painters and sculptors concerned very much with isolating the aesthetic content, and this is a preoccupation which seems most likely to result in good rather than great art. But I think this is a situation which has very possibly passed its creative peak, for the exploration of is-ness, 'concreteness', may have very definite limitations.

In the new situation which is beginning to make its presence visible, analysis will play a less important part than synthesis, and to this, historical awareness may well contribute a great deal. 'Modernism' is going to be replaced by post-modernism, a widening instead of a narrowing; and in this the fear of knowledge will be replaced at least to some extent by drives towards comprehensiveness and perhaps by an era of greatness as well as goodness. I must remind you that I speak as a working sculptor and not as an art historian; that I speak from what I feel and not from anything that I can claim to know.

Now, not only can history increase the breadth of a man's comprehension; I also believe that the pressures of history are so strong today that they cannot be totally resisted, and that partial resistance is emotionally dangerous.

If you can find a place for him to live, secure from everything that is going on in the rest of the world, by all means leave the savage alone, and his work, within the limitations of his horizon, may well be vital. But if he is to be exposed at all, then let him be properly exposed to the full breadth of contemporary awareness. Let him realize himself as but a part of the whole of evolving nature, and at least it will help him to avoid the sin of hubris. At least it will develop his sympathy for all other living creatures and enable him to respond fully to the condition or predicament of being human; at least from then on his drives may not be merely personal, egocentric, flat-earth ones.

In a very practical way exposure to history will also protect you against the many gnomic utterances which may be imposed on you; statements the profundity of which is dependent upon their obscurity. For instance,

Less is more, or *Truth is beauty and beauty truth*. Such utterances are themselves works of art, and can contribute greatly to the richness of human experience, but as magical incantations they can do untold harm.

Additionally, history can protect you against what I call art/hate syndromes, similar tumid mental growths. A particularly virulent example of this disease I would describe as the art/nature/morality syndrome.

If a study of history can be said to give protection, it can also act as a great stimulant, particularly in relation to the immediate past. To see the forms of 'modernism' in a historical context is to recognize their validity as well as their shortcomings. It will help you not only to avoid the dissipation of your energies in anti/historical struggles, but it will also alert you to the possibilities of what goes on. Your past will breed your future anyway, I know, but make historical study a greater part of your past and the result may well be a more dynamic future.

And now to come to the question of the alleged dangers of historical knowledge. In my opinion there is only one which deserves serious thought: the widespread contemporary belief that knowledge can destroy emotional drive. To some extent I believe this to be a possibility. Although it is a subject which is in the province of the psychologist, my view, for what it is worth, is that in certain circumstances particular creative emotional tensions may be dissipated by learning, but that it is a matter which is more apparent than real. This is a widespread attitude, due to a misunderstanding of psychology—a belief that the subconscious mind is only vaguely subconscious, and is really quite accessible if you think about it a bit! This just is not true; the human psyche is virtually impenetrable to any normal intellectual onslaught. The good Lord provides every working artist with a remarkably strong electrified fence around his genius—one in fact which is so strong in many cases that even the displayed evidence of his own creative past is insufficient to put him off his stride. For it is certain that our objectives in life are emotionally selected, not intellectually arrived at. Emotion selects our ends, and the intellect provides the means to them.

I have said that a study of history will give you some protection against the debilitating effect of the art-hate syndrome, and that it will enable you to steer your way past some of the great gnomic utterances left and often discarded by other artists, which can stand like bollards in the way of your evolution. Medically a syndrome may be defined as a complex of morbid symptoms which occur together, constituting a distinct clinical picture. I have borrowed the term from medical practice because it seems to me that a very similar condition can occur where drives originally directed towards resolving tensions by painting and sculpture become confused, obscured, and largely replaced by drives towards quite different ends without this change of direction being accepted. The result is at best a confused pattern of motivation, and at worst complete paralysis of the creative will. Typical examples suggest creative drives towards craftsmanship instead of art, science instead of art: morality, objectivity, security, position, prestige or a mixture of all these.

Creative drives acting through minds which have comprehended history as an intelligible pattern are not in my view so prone to decay into uncreative eccentricity. An awareness of history will safeguard you.

The virulence of the art-hate syndrome stems from its being a quarter-truth rather than a damned lie. To take a typical example, which I call the art-nature-morality syndrome: it would be foolish to deny that morality has no place in art. Of course it has; but this syndrome is a case of the part becoming greater than the whole.

The experience of coming into contact with an acute sufferer may be described something like this: the first thing you will realize is that his general bearing is either markedly manic or depressive; symptoms, however, of one and the same emotional condition. In the depressive form he is revealing his fundamental apathy, his indifference, his feeling that art is not really worth it. In the manic condition he still feels fundamentally the same, but is out to compensate for it at all costs, and consequently he over-compensates. In either case he will sooner or later reveal himself: his attention will be taken by some natural object, perhaps a tree, perhaps a bone, perhaps an animal. His eye gleaming, he will say, 'Isn't that beautiful, isn't that really wonderful!' but before you have time to answer he will go on: 'Now if only Mr X's painting could be like that, then it would be the real thing!' At that moment you know your man; he has lost the will to create, and has become a nature lover instead, and with all the emotional strength at his command he now loves nature even as he hates art. In his suffering he is unable to realize that the beauty of art and the beauty of nature are totally different experiences; that while a painting or sculpture is most certainly a part of nature in so far as it has been produced as a part of total evolution, its news value is different.

A bone or a rock is simply what it is, but a painting or a sculpture, apart from being what it is, is also a statement made by a man, a mark. A gesture, a gesture of approval, or a *cri de cœur*, but whichever it is, it is still a man's mark.

The symptoms of this sad case include:

1. Either total artistic inactivity, or extensive but erratic, even hysterical, production in an ever-widening variety of styles.

2. A hypercritical attitude to contemporary art of all kinds, accompanied by approving references to the greatness and beauty of nature and/or approving references to the art of the distant past.

3. Constant critical references to the lack of dedication of all contemporary artists (except himself). The opinion that only the dead artists were free from common human failings such as greed, lust, and envy.

All this is in fact a loss of creative will, a replacement

28

of art satisfactions by nature love, a replacement of a love of art in all its amorality by a love of morality itself, accompanied withal by vast deception.

Man probably is vile; I do not deny it. But man's art is nevertheless the only art there is, and the love of art is not to be replaced by another without destroying creative will.

In life you will meet many substitute drives masquerading as art; and while exposure to history will certainly not prevent the decay of a man's emotional thrust, it may at least produce a degree of intellectual honesty sufficient to enable him to avoid a living hell of self-deception. To be condemned to death in a fortnight concentrates the mind wonderfully, and to be condemned to an awareness of history is not so very different. By the way, it is as well to remember that it is not merely Picasso and Cézanne who have condemned the Royal Academy, but the whole of history.

In comparison, the dangers from the gnomic utterances are perhaps much less serious, but these mystical oversimplifications are certainly something more than mere nuisances. At least they demand a détour. Let me remind you of a few:

> I do not seek, I find.
> Beauty is truth—truth beauty
> Sculpture is architecture.
> Art is artificial.
> Less is more.

Although one of these is my own contribution, I

penitently accept its egocentric origins. You should be warned of these half-truths, and history is the best warning I know.

I would like to say something here about the last one. Currently, 'less is more' tends to be attributed to the original mind of Mondrian, but its origin is far more ancient. The philosopher William of Occam is credited with the precept, 'It is vain to do with more what can be done with fewer' as far back as the fourteenth century.

While Occam was concerned with philosophical investigation, the less-is-more doctrine is most clearly seen today as an aspect of puritanism, even of masochism. It is in fact a moral assertion with considerable appeal to the protestantism of Western Europe and North America. It is not really an informative statement but an emotive one, and the appeal of the concept 'less is more' to a man like Mondrian is perfectly easy to understand in the light of what we know of his psychological make-up. For the act of denying the physical sensual universe obviously gave him a positive masochistic pleasure, and his painting towards the end of his life was an affirmation of self-restraint and self-denial. But if 'less is more' was tailor-made for Mondrian, can you reasonably suppose that it would be as natural an outfit for a quite different man? Having supper with him some eighteen months ago it transpired that he had just returned from a number of weeks in Italy looking at Botticellis, Masaccios, Pieros, and so on, and I could not help feeling that his concentration on a relatively narrow band of expression had atrophied his ability to enjoy experiences which for many of us are the height of aesthetic pleasure. This man, you see, was concentrating more and more on less and less, with the result that the fullness and balance of Italian painting had become for him a mere wallowing in sensuality. A Botticelli Venus had become in fact a Hollywood cutie on a television screen. On very short acquaintance it is, I know, unfair to claim that here is a man who has passionately received a gnomic statement which, suited to another, nevertheless fits him very ill indeed; but I can only tell you that far from revelling in his abstemiousness as might St Francis, he conveyed, to me at least, a sense of deprivation. Among your acquaintances I am sure you have often recognized a man flying the wrong colours. If so, take it from me he is a casualty of under-exposure; a man whose development is going to be delayed, and whom history in its widest sense would help to recognize himself.

Now I want briefly to discuss one or two aspects of contemporary art which may indicate the kind of historical speculation which I regard as appropriate to a working artist: the kind of speculation which clarifies, releases and consequently stimulates.

A long long time ago, in fact in the year in which I was born, Kandinsky was actively painting non-figurative compositions, and ever since then, debilitating argumentation has gone on over the question of whether a low degree of figuration can result in good art. The people who have argued most actively about this have tended to take up extreme positions, that is to say, on the one hand it is claimed that non-figuration is a release, that it provides artistic freedom, that it shows the way to the summit of human artistic achievement, while on the other hand one hears the moaning and grumbling of those who would have preserved art in alcohol from 1850 onwards.

But history will give you a perspective within which these pointless arguments can be seen for what they are. For good or ill, non-figuration is as natural a product of the twentieth century as is the rocket, and comprehending this you will avoid the dissipation of energy in useless warfare. For the drives towards non-figuration such as those of contemporary primitivism, even I think surrealism, are exactly those to be expected in a century where for the first time the old anthropocentric pattern of belief has at last finally and completely crumbled. Galileo, Darwin and Freud have done their job, and 1961 is their offspring. Take cognizance of this, and you will not need to go very deeply into psychology to see that man has become an orphan—has lost his traditional centre, and must at last make do with himself. In default of a great, good, and beneficent deity which he has destroyed, he directs his hatred inwardly against his own image. Although man has at last destroyed God, he seeks at the same time to comfort himself with a surrogate mother, an artifact in place of the breast which has been withdrawn from him. Art, now, is object *and* symbol.

And what of the man who, feeling this loss, has no means to come to terms with the situation? His predicament is awful; and nowhere is this to be more clearly seen than in the writings of the German historian Hans Sedlmayr. In his violent, almost pathological, attack on contemporary art is revealed not the shortcomings of art but Professor Sedlmayr's own predicament: the predicament of a man who bewails the decline of an authoritarian structure, a pyramid with God at the top, his rulers a little way down, and we, the scum of the earth, at the base.

I do not wish to bore you with his diatribes; I merely refer him to your attention if you want to investigate a pathological case of God-loss. For Sedlmayr is the victim of Galileo, of Newton, and of Freud. His book *Verlust der Mitte* is the *cri de cœur* of a slave whose master has deserted him, and who with horror contemplates the void in which he finds himself: a void in which his comfortable anthropocentric universe has been swallowed up; a void in which the earth goes round the sun, man himself is but a part of the total evolutionary process, and the possessor not of a divine spirit but of a mental anatomy only once removed from that of an ape.

Those of us who are prepared to tolerate existence in a post-Galilean, post-Darwinian, post-Freudian world, are nevertheless in some measure suffering from the same misery as Sedlmayr, but unlike him we have to

33

some extent found the means of salvation, and our painting and sculpture are an aspect of this.

Some of us have sought to create convincing beauty outside man's image, to abstract aesthetic content from its biological origins. Others attempt, perhaps even succeed in making a coherence, a unity, out of fragmentation itself.

Having no mother to symbolize, many have attempted to produce actual concrete, mother material —not a symbol for the breast, but the breast itself; others to withdraw to a dream world wherein to enjoy the delights experienced before the fall.

The mother figure has let us down, and we, her miserable children, are in process of taking our revenge; but even though we vent our anger on her through ourselves, we do not, on this side of the lunatic asylum, go the whole hog. We sneer, we splinter, and we fragmentate, but even as we destroy we also build. Yet it seems to me that the first phase of man's contemporary hell is passing, and you and succeeding generations will have creative drives which have been denied to those of us who have been at work during the last fifty years. To prophesy is dangerous, but I would hazard a guess that the dirt-scatterers, the disembowellers, and the disappearing-man merchants will not be so characteristic of art in twenty years from now.

A concomitant of the new situation is, as might be expected, the search for new mother-gods to fill the emotional vacuum. Already many have sought comfort in the apparent certainties of scientific knowledge, and this quest for a new god manifests itself in many ways, not least of which is a preoccupation with a phony dramatized science worship; an emotive attitude to science, with science as a new mother figure, science the saviour, science the Messiah. It has already had many prophets, Moholy-Nagy, the futurists Antoine Pevsner, Gabo; they are legion, but the god they worship is I believe a false god, and one already in 1961 discredited in the eyes of many thinking men. For science is but a system devised by man as a means of comprehending his environment—a model-building technique, nothing more. There are no gods, there can be no gods, and in fact there never were any. If twentieth-century art has helped a little to assuage the personal void for many artists, and through their works vicariously for many others, then it is still functioning as a socially meaningful activity in spite of the pessimists and their constant talk of the great schism between the artist and his public. Perhaps *au fond* things today are less different than they may seem to be.

Three: The Importance of Means

THIS group of lectures is supposed to be a survey of ideas relevant to creative growth, not a detailed study of particular problems such as carving or casting, colour-mixing or lithographic techniques. These have their proper place in the studio. The way I want to consider technology this afternoon is at the level at which it differentiates the plastic arts from those involving other material means ... music which employs sound, poetry which uses words, and so on.

The expressiveness of an art-object is the product of its idea acting through its material and manifesting itself as form: this form is the product of the most complete interaction—neither the idea nor the material has any significance alone.

When we describe a painting or a sculpture as literary we do not mean precisely that it expresses no more than would be possible by means of words—any Victorian blue sky communicates at least something not entirely analysable verbally. We mean rather that the artist fails to make us respond to the way he has organized his forms and handled his material. The way

36

a painter 'slaps the stuff down', or a sculptor chops at plaster, is for us a most important element in an aesthetic experience.

I think one can go even further. We demand today that a very great part of our experience shall come from our consciousness of the work as an object—its *isness*.

I suggested last week that this might well be due to the work's comforting us—in child psychology, corresponding to the breast which has been withdrawn; in wider terms, comforting us in our godless, purpose-less void—if I properly understand Adrian Stokes.

Other explanations, of course, may be given—for instance, that the artist is reacting away from photo-graphy, that in today's machine-made world we are starved of handmadeness, that the collector enjoys the evidence before his eyes of the artist's hand at work, and so on. But with these explanations or others the net result is the same: we are conscious that through their material the plastic arts can communicate something beyond the possibilities of discourse, and rightly or wrongly we value this something very greatly. Those painters and sculptors who confine themselves to techniques aimed at the suppression of their material seem to us to lack the kind of vitality we have come to expect.

How long this supersensitivity to the concrete object will last, no one can say; but while it does, the student's need for every possible technical facility is of the greatest importance. Mucking about with paint and canvas, plaster and bronze, is a very expensive business, and the possibility of many unsuccessful experiments and the need for working large to see what will happen as well as small to see what will happen, means that a society preoccupied with *l'art concret* needs a very deep pocket. It is no good expecting a painter to anticipate on 100 square inches his chances on 100 square feet if the actuality of the object is his preoccupation. Neither can a sculptor anticipate much of value in respect of working in iron, by making clay models. For as long as this phase lasts the student must have equipment and materials provided on an altogether more lavish scale than a hundred years ago, and the sooner educational bodies realize this the better.

In the not so distant past, surface texture was used largely for decorative or illustrative purposes, while further back in time its expressive possibilities were obviously unconsciously felt in a way much closer to the present day. This may well have been for similar reasons—the close comfort of the object as opposed to the distance of the illusion. Be this as it may, I believe that the artist's enjoyment in handling his materials can be a vital element in his life. I have often felt that the drive to be a painter rather than a sculptor (or vice versa) is generated primarily at this wash-tub level. For the painter is the man who can bear the stink of turpentine and the horror of cleaning paint brushes, while the sculptor must be above all the little boy who enjoys messing about with clay and plaster. The painter's mess is out there—at brush-length away; the sculptor's is close in, and all around him.

38

But if material is to the painter what words are to the poet, what happens when it runs away with him? How important in the long run, perhaps, is this very contemporary preoccupation going to be? The pleasures of smearing paint and handling clay are obviously comforting, and closely allied to, if not substitutes for, erotic activity; and the singular enjoyment of making can sometimes obscure any attention to making-expressive. Painting and sculpture may then become entirely therapeutic—craftsmanship for its own sake. Good for the artist, if he can be called such, but of little value or concern to anyone else.

In large international *art et lumière* festivals it is possible to find acres of painting and sculpture which, while one hopes they were very good for their creators, seem little more than therapeutic objects. I do not think this suggests that there is more bad art made today than in the recent past, only that present-day criteria are more difficult to apply, and consequently more rubbish is exhibited.

Where then do we draw the line? If Brancusi was the first sculptor, since the invention of art in 1850 to exploit the object as an expressive device, where does Frankenstein's monster begin to take over? Where does the tail begin to wag the dog? I suggest, at the point where the manipulation of material becomes an exclusive end, or a qualification for membership of the contemporary academy—the *style tourisme*! And how, you may ask, do we determine this point? The answer is: we can't, objectively. We shall have to wait until the

39

quite distant future before we can decide which of the comforters of the twentieth century are merely Alma Tademas and Leightons. Until then, we depend on our subjective sensibility, and that alone. All I can do is warn you, and ask you, as you develop, to apply the same questioning response to this, perhaps the most characteristic aspect of present-day art, as you doubtless already do to the Pre-Raphaelites.

If great art is to be defined as art which provides the highest level of emotional experience for the greatest number of people, over the longest span of time, it seems to me axiomatic that the elevation of one aspect of an art to a position of overriding importance may well result in a narrower spectrum of content, so that a sculpture—for instance by Giacometti—which may appear tailor-made to contemporary anxiety, must contain a great deal more as well, if it is not going to become a period piece of 1961 taste when the cultural climate alters. But, although the awful prognostications of Wyndham Lewis's demon of progress do not frighten me any more than Sedlmayr's void, nevertheless I can see the extent to which the preoccupations of those whom I regard as the greater artists of this century seem to operate diagonally across the super-fashionable movements. Reflecting, but never becoming completely absorbed in the over-simplifications of the recognized movements, the artist as an individual has got to be greater than the 'movement' to which he belongs.

À propos art as a 'comforter', I cannot resist drawing

your attention to the peculiar connections I feel it has with eroticism. There is something here which at first sight looks like a paradox. Consider:

> The artist's physical engagement with paint and plaster has much in common with sexual play.

> Making the material read, making it actual, results in a bravura of texture.

> Yet erotic art is characteristically smooth, naked rather than nude. Huxley's Brave New World Girls were 'ever so pneumatic'!

Perhaps one sees here symbolic substitutes for sex being replaced by physical sexual substitutes. Conceivably, mother-directed sexuality replacing girl-friend sexuality.

Comfort, closeness (for only in things near to us are we really conscious of texture) replacing dream-quality smoothness. Teddy bears, nice and cosy, replacing Gogol's wife, replaced by the life-sized inflatable rubber doll Gogol made as a convenient substitute for a real wife. Dubuffet replacing Delvaux, placental mess replacing Dali's (or Ingres) pneumatic surface illusions.

This replacement of the girl-friend relationship by the mother relationship with all its Œdipus complex controls available, perhaps enables the artist to come to closer grips with sexual experience without being accused of pornography. For society accepts practically anything if it can be called maternity. Post-orgasmic imagery suits a mass culture, because it is seen as a stabilizing social force, not a disruptive one.

I also wonder if this mother-sex art is not only what the godless void demands, but is also custom-built for ageing artists, the blurred touch of the old man replacing the indecent clarity of youth. Compare, for instance, the young with the old Picasso. Think about this, and do not involve yourself in old man's art before you have to!

This matter of concreteness is worth considering briefly in connection with the other arts—music, poetry, and architecture. It would be nice and straightforward if one could say: 'From the middle of the nineteenth century, when Huxley, Darwin, and the precursors of Freud were attacking established belief at every level, artists, architects, musicians, and poets began to manufacture god-mother objects! But history isn't as tidy as that, and it seems to me that other explanations for the is-ness of modern architecture, the truth to material of the sculptors, the word preoccupation of James Joyce and Gertrude Stein, and the *musique concrète* of the last decade, need to be considered.

What explanations are offered?

In architecture, we are told that the technology of the Industrial Revolution provided the stimuli which generated the new architectural forms. In music and poetry experimentation, deriving from an awareness of scientific techniques, has been said to be responsible. I suggest that you ask yourselves how far this may be true,

42

and that you consider whether perhaps only modern painting and sculpture have seriously answered the deeper needs of the situation with a viable art form. Becket follows Joyce, no-one follows Stein. *Musique concrète* has not, as yet anyway, contributed a great deal to human experience, and architecture seems to be rushing away from functionalism fast towards the neo-fascism of Eero Saarinen.

In the last 150 years a new element has appeared in visual art, and anyone who has experienced seeing their own work in the cinema or on a television screen, will know what I mean when I say that although much is lost, there is at least something gained.

First, there is an increased suspension of disbelief; excessive familiarity with the image is prevented because it isn't in fact there in the room with you.

Second, even in the best-regulated cinemas there is an element of flicker, a touch of movement, communicated by the technical device. By the way, I wonder if you have ever noticed how an old 78 r.p.m. record gives something of its own speed to the recording?

Third, even where the object shown does not itself move, the film or T.V. programme does. You know, even as you look, that what you are seeing will soon be replaced by something else without any action on your part.

You are seeing an art of movement, created in the dimension of time as well as space, and in my view resisting disbelief in a way no static object can.

Hitchcock's *Psycho* pulls you into its horror more

effortlessly than can any painting, and if any of you saw *Payroll* you will have experienced, in the episode where a 15-ton lorry repeatedly bashes into an armoured truck until the truck cracks open, an experience of action of a far more dynamic order than any New York painting.

The fact is that the cinema demands much less cultivation of sensibility than do painting and sculpture. Almost any film achieves a dynamic effect at least equivalent to the greatest paintings and sculptures. But please note that I have said dynamic effect. I have not said that any film provides a greater total emotional experience, over a period of time.

When Kandinsky began to create non-figurative paintings in the early part of the century, the cinema already existed in rudimentary form. He and the futurists in Italy reacted, not only to the time-idea, already a dimension of music, but to the first conjunction of actual movement and form in a visual art object. But what Kandinsky said about painting would have made much more expressive sense if he had been working in the cinema. For it seems to me that his colour-music theories, with their attendant preoccupation with low figuration, are much less valid where divorced from time.

I was first made forcibly aware of this when walking through a large exhibition of non-figurative painting. As a whole I seemed to derive a pleasure which I found impossible to experience from any single object, and I came to the conclusion that this was probably due to the fact that I was not enjoying individual pictures so much as a sequence. *Time*, the material of music and the cinema, had in this instance entered into my experience of the plastic arts. Most of you will know Giedion's view of this in connection with architecture. From that time onwards I have become more and more convinced that the true apotheosis of non-figurative painting might be found not in the individual picture but in a sequence of pictures. Just as I can find a simple pattern of formal colour relationships relatively boring after a few minutes, so I would find the continuous repetition of three or four musical notes. But in the same way as I find a musical sequence created in time a moving and exciting experience, so I imagine, I would enjoy an extended series of non-figurative compositions serially organized. The sequence prevents one from demanding too much of any single unit. Of course, a number of non-figurative film sequences have already been made, and I think have been largely successful.

I do not doubt that the invention of photography has already had a profound effect on painting, but I believe we are, at this moment, seeing in contemporary painting a large-scale impact of the cinema, different from that which resulted in Futurism.

There is never just one reason for anything, and if what I say now suggests that the reason I give replaces what I have already said about the void, then I shall certainly be misunderstood. In my view many of the current forms of painting, the preoccupation with attack, the movement of the artist's brush, the blurring

45

of shapes, the a-focal nature of compositional arrange-
ment, and the frequent detachment of colour from form,
represent an effort on the part of the painter to compete
with the dynamics of the cinema and television. These
have so put the screw on him that he has tended to
forget that his means are limited to the dimensions of
space. But this is a situation which *may* not continue.
Already 'action' is not such a key word as it was five
years ago. At that time the critics not only drew our
attention to the action expressiveness of the New York
painters, but naïvely implied that the pictures were the
actual consequence of the painter going berserk with a
pot of paint. We now know—as we should have
realized all along—that even in America art is artificial.
I know Hartung, and how he works, and I am certain
that his premeditated care is largely characteristic of
others producing dynamic effects.

Action painting is the art of premeditated spon-
taneity, and the bravura of much contemporary sculpture is by no means the simple consequence of slinging
mud from a distance of six feet.

My guess is, that to survive, painting and sculpture
will return to preoccupations which are more naturally
their own province, to do things which the cinema
cannot. Anyway the comfort-object is probably the
better for its static isness. Mother is waiting behind
baby's chair, she won't run away, and you can't
switch her off!

But consider the cinema, investigate the part it may
play in your creative development, but if necessary, be

brave enough to admit that what you may really want to do is to make film. If this is so, be ruthless enough to act on your convictions.

If the cinema has been playing the devil with painting, in a slightly different way I think the pub-lished photograph has been doing quite a lot to sculp-ture. When I went to the Picasso exhibition last sum-mer, I was very much struck by the feeling that I had seen it all before. This did not mean that I was bored or fed-up; I didn't feel that it was 'old hat' or irrelevant. It was in no sense the reaction that I had had to the Braque show earlier. I came to the conclusion that it was due to the particular character of Picasso's con-tribution to the twentieth century: a contribution quite as much of ideas as of objects, and that this kind of contribution transmits very well through the medium of photographic reproduction.

Consider in contrast a typical work by Picasso and one by Monet. The power of Picasso lies very often in the idea say for instance the double profile, an idea easily distributed throughout the world by photo-graphs. But the strength of a Monet lies in its concrete existence, its isness, as a rectangle of canvas covered with magical paint. At most, a photograph of the *Water Lilies* merely encourages you to make a great effort to see the original.

Now as objects sculptures are awkward things; they are often heavy, often bulky, and sometimes very spiky—they are not so very easy to move around; but during the last fifteen years there has been an enormous development in the photographing of sculpture, and the distribution of books of photographs.

Obviously this sculptography can give genuine aesthetic pleasure. The work of Bill Brandt, recently published, is the same kind of art, although he uses a living model and a wide-angle lens instead of a sculpture and a wide-angle lens. But it can also be a form of rather dubious persuasion. On the cover of the *Motor* last week was an advertisement for a Vauxhall Victor, a picture of the car in what was intended as a delightful setting—mountains, blue sea, laughing happy people. The caption was revealing: Own a wonderful world, own a Vauxhall. In our dreams perhaps, when we buy a Renault Dauphine, we buy the blonde which goes with it, or nearer home you get British sculpture and the landscape as well.

For good or ill the sculptor is bound to respond to this situation, and I believe the effect, at times, has not been altogether desirable. This is serious, because while sculpture-photography can give considerable pleasure, its contribution is bound to be of a rather narrow kind. Great emphasis is placed on two things; the pictorial effect, and textural vitality. The danger is that if sculptures continue to be created for exhibition in photographic form, much which properly belongs to sculpture itself and can only be expressed through sculpture, may become lost. The pictorial emphasis tends to break up the sculptural object, because in producing photographic excitement a pictorial spread of form becomes necessary. There are severe limitations

48

in the photographic possibilities of a single standing figure, say a *Willendorf Venus*, while there are considerable photographic possibilities in Moore's double-sectioned reclining figures, or my own figures in space. Texturally, there are photographic possibilities in many works which are not, I think, as viable in terms of the actual sculpture, and this situation can be found occurring all over Europe.

This is a rather different case from what I have been talking about in connection with the effect of the cinema on painting. The sculptor is not in fact competing with the still photograph, but making use of an additional means of expression. How far this process will go I do not know; I have often thought it would be exciting to create a series of sculptures with the intention that they should only exist in photographs. But somehow my attachment to the actual object has prevented my attempting to carry this out. One thing, however, is certain, and that is that what is good for photography is by no means equally good for sculpture. For the contribution that sculpture can best make derives from its existence being bound up with an objective, tangible lump of material: something that you meet as you meet another human being, something which is actual physical matter, its organization being such that appreciation of it extends beyond illusion into actuality. If I succeed in concocting a mixture of wax and plaster so that it becomes a sort of female material, then what I am doing is not exercising my abilities to perform the same kind of conjuring trick as happens on an

49

illusionistic canvas. It is still a conjuring trick, I agree, but of a very different order. For the perceptive mechanism we bring into play in order to enjoy a sculpture is much more than purely optical, although I am told on good authority that what one tends to regard as a tactile experience is usually in point of fact a visual one. We must not forget that we have two eyes, and hands, and methods of sensing the presence of solid objects near us, whereas the camera has but one eye and nothing else.

In a photograph, a knife-cut, filled with white powder, or a residue of moulding material, can read as the most powerful thing recognized. But not so in sculpture; and I am convinced that in some ways the better a piece of sculpture, the more impossible it is to convey what is really important about it in a photograph. The part the camera can play, and shall be allowed to play in the creative development of a sculptor, is worth most serious consideration. The one-eyed box can tell you a great deal about certain aspects of your work, particularly the power of your idea, but it represents a danger as well as a challenge.

Four: Study

THE question of artmanship—by which I mean received technique—is a difficult one to discuss seriously without becoming solemn, or involved in a sort of university union debate on the motion 'Should art schools be abolished?' But since I am concerned in these lectures with the general problem of creative development, the case for the traditional art school has to be seriously examined. I suggest we clear the ground a little by agreeing that the nub of the question is the life-class; that outside this, any art school is simply a polytechnic providing training in technical skills. The case for telling a potential artist that he can mix plaster with water, or buy more or less permanent colours in tubes, is not, I think, debatable. Neither need we argue the value of a student's mixing with other people who happen to believe (or at least act as if they believed) that making paintings or sculptures is a worthwhile occupation. So we are faced with the question of the life-class, so called, and this alone.

I begin by asking whether the life-class can be justified empirically. For instance, can we recognize any difference between the art of those who have been exposed to life-class teaching or its equivalent, and those who have not, and if we can, is it a difference of kind, or quality, or both? Again, is the situation today so different from that of the past, that even if we conclude empirically that the life-class has at times made better artists, the value of such a conclusion is worthless *vis-à-vis* the foreseeable future?

I said in the first lecture that I believed in general that art schools produced different *kinds* of artist, but not necessarily better or worse ones. But it has been argued by some people, that the Douanier Rousseau would have been a greater artist had he been exposed to art school experience at an early age, and I cannot refute this proposition. I can only refuse to accept it. When I contemplate what might have been lost to the world had the Douanier received, for instance, a drawing system based on imaginary sight lines intersecting an assumed picture plane thirty inches from his nose, I am simply appalled. Similarly I have heard it said that So and So would be a better artist had he been a less good student. These are hypotheses which get no-one anywhere. For I do not think we can claim to know enough about the effects of school exposure, let alone aesthetic values, to be more dogmatic than to say that we cannot abolish the life-class on the empirical evidence available.

The second question: There have been, during the last forty years, important artists who have claimed that traditional life-class study is a waste of time, that the modern manifestations of art need to be so different from those of the past that the old tradition, whereby a student spent long hours of his career struggling with the problem of making pictorial and sculptural statements about the model standing in front of him, has nothing to offer. To be frank, I think there is something in this point of view, but not much, for basically I do not consider the so-called modern art revolution to be in retrospect a revolution in anything other than name; nor do I consider the problem of being an artist today as in any profound way different from that of being an artist 500 or 5000 years ago.

I know we are experiencing what appears to be, on the surface, a new world—a world of aeroplanes, of rockets, of psychological techniques for examining the human mind, of the development of ever more complex machines designed to do operations previously carried out by human beings. Huxley's *Brave New World* and Orwell's *1984*, are already here in many respects. This has led many to maintain that everything is different, a belief sometimes engendered by a subjective admiration for the idea of modernism, but it is a mistaken belief, for what is really new is only certain aspects of man's environment, not the character of man himself.

We experience today life within a double framework; on the one hand the rapidly evolving man-made environment, and on the other, the altogether slower evolutionary rhythm of the biological creature. You or I differ very little from the men of ancient Greece or the upper palaeolithic period. The brain, the bones, and the teeth of Gagarin are in no profound way dissimilar from the brain, the bones, and the teeth of a man of ancient Egypt.

An artist reacts to what is, and those who have said that everything is different, are lying. But equally let me remind you that those who have said that everything is the same are also lying. The academy of the Venice *biennale* is an academy of one-wheeled vehicles, but the academy of Burlington House is equally ill-equipped.

I do not therefore believe it is possible to make a case for abolishing or preserving the art school, either on the ground that it makes worse or better artists, or that the world today is so very different from the past. Primarily, I justify the art school on the lack of an objective case against it. If this view is too negative for your tastes, I am sorry, but I do not think you will find a more substantial case, however hard you try, and to be frank, the positive case I now offer rests simply on my personal belief. Although I consider my argument persuasive, it cannot be the same thing as one based on empirical evidence.

Now, if the term life-class means anything, it means a class where something is alleged to be taught. What? Art? Can art be taught? No, because you cannot demonstrate how to get something 'right' unless you can claim to recognize 'rightness' with a high degree of certainty, and in addition communicate information about the qualities a work must have in order to be right—or wrong.

This is not the eighteenth century, the world of Addison, or Walpole, or William Chambers, and we have lost the innocent naïvety of Reynolds or even Voltaire. We can no longer approach the problem of painting or poetry with a received conception of *correctness*, a prefabricated aesthetic yardstick. No tutor, no critic can, in my opinion, claim to be doing more than exercising his very subjective preferences. Undoubtedly there are basic principles, but who can claim to recognize them for others to follow without question?

All this, you of course realize, is tied up with the problem of objectifying aesthetic values, but I do not want to spend time on that question just now, because I hope to say something on the general subject of aesthetics in my last lecture. However, if anyone feels I am making an unnecessary bogy out of this problem, I will undertake to disabuse him of that idea in under five minutes.

But if the tutor cannot undertake to show a student how to get things aesthetically right, what can he teach? I maintain that the student can be helped to study. The question of the art school has now been reduced to that of the life-class, and the life-class to that of study, so I can now disclose my great revelation. Study is what, being students, you should do in a studio. Application of the mind and hand, thoughtful attention, meditation; so the dictionary says. But what should you study? How can study help you, and what are the risks you will run?

I have, I fear, to continue in a pedantic way, and

55

stress that I am talking about an activity consequent upon an intention. I am talking about intending to study, not intending to make art, and about the consequence of intending to study, not of intending to make art. This has to be clearly understood if I am to convince you that the act of study is a worthwhile one, deserving your respect and devotion, for I have at the same time to convince you that it is only a means to an end and not an end in itself.

Now although making art is concerned with making 'good' or 'right' or 'expressive' for you, study, as I define it, is directed towards objectivity. I say directed towards objectivity rather than objective, for in no activity, least of all art, can you honestly claim 'objectivity'. In the life-class you will perhaps have better opportunities of acquiring various technical skills than under less organized conditions, but I would not justify a period of your life spent in study if this were the only contribution.

I believe it should primarily be thought of as a means of furnishing the raw materials of creation. A blind and deaf man, with no tactile sensibility, would not have much opportunity of collecting experience with which to create. Put crudely, what comes out has first to go in, and objective study is an intensive method of taking in, taking in the forms of which plastic experience is made up; of the animal kingdom in general, of all growing organisms, visible and microscopic, and of inorganic matter, for these are the vocabulary of the plastic arts and the subjective rearrangement of nature is the basis of their practice. Creativity is not origination except in terms of bringing together (bisociation is Koestler's word); the bringing together in a plastic unity of elements not previously comprehended in a common context. In all the arts a vocabulary is necessary. Tutuola only had Pidgin English available, so *The Palm Wine Drinkard and the Dead Malt Tapster* is created in terms of Pidgin English. It is obvious that no poet can use the French language as a creative medium if he only comprehends the existence of German. Equally the artist must concern himself with acquiring a vocabulary, and the only question is where? In the life-class or in the street, or in a night spot in Berlin? In other words, in an emotionally neutral setting or under circumstances charged with emotion? I believe both.

I do not, I think, need to justify the value of emotionally charged experience, for it is surely the indisputable material of creative energy. But what about the neutral atmosphere of the life-class? Well, for one thing it will not always be emotively neutral; yet even where it is, the artist will acquire another spectrum of experience, itself valuable. A quieter, more detached view, the view a little perhaps of a lizard blinking in the sun. A slow-growing comprehension of things making their presence felt in minute increments, a passionless unfolding of secrets. Something quite different from the electrifying flash of an emotionally dynamic sudden perception. Of course this can decay, and often does, into a general lowering of the level of your emotional intensity. But this will be your misfortune. Regrettable; but there is little that anyone can do about it. You take a calculated risk.

And to be more precise; with what kind of aims should a student concern himself? And what are sufficiently objective pursuits to make possible a useful rapport between student and tutor?

The anatomical organization not merely of human beings but of animals, plants, bacteria, crystals, rocks, machines and buildings. The simplicity and complexity of their forms, their articulation, the disposition of stresses and strains in living and non-living structures. Recognition of the qualities of things; their hardness and softness, heaviness and lightness, tautness and slackness, smoothness and roughness. Recognition of unities and similarities, rhythms and analogues, differences. The character of space, the definition of space, the penetration of things into space. The nature of illumination, its determination of what we see (as opposed to what we know otherwise than by vision from a static point in space). The news-value of colour. The way our reading of experience is controlled by the means by which we perceive.

At every stage the student will find his human subjectivity getting in the way of his apprehension of reality. But meeting this problem is itself a most valuable pursuit, and it is one where a second pattern of senses—the tutor's, can be most valuable.

Here I beg you to give thought to your intention, to decide as far as you can what you are studying, and communicate this, as far as you can, to the tutor. And in case something or other carries you away from detachment into a realm of emotional expressiveness, do not claim objective preoccupation unless you feel you honestly have good grounds for doing so. The sight of student and tutor talking at completely different levels, if not at cross purposes, is spiritually offensive. Life is too short to waste time in misunderstanding when a little honest effort can often avoid it.

Insist on exploring the widest range of techniques you can, but at all times preserve an openness of mind towards them. Be passionately involved, but also nurse your scepticism; it it your lifeline as an artist. I say this particularly to you girls, because in general I think you lack a sufficiently sceptical response to ideas handed you on a plate by tutors.

Cultivate your powers of belief, but do not, to begin with at least, permit yourselves to believe in any one doctrine too much. Do not allow yourselves too early in your career to decide that this material is your *métier* and no other, or that the way to draw is thus and not thus. Beware of getting yourself into a closed circuit where means and ends have become so interrelated that your activity becomes a sort of higher mathematics. The arithmetic of study is good, but not, I believe, its philosophy.

Combine a capacity to see anything you have undertaken through to the end, with keeping yourself constantly on the move. In sculpture, for instance, work large and very large, but also small and very small. Discover for yourselves the dangers of mere copyism which come with full-size working, or the superficiality of smallness to save time. Realize that when you change scale you compel yourself to think, to recreate rather than to imitate.

But what of the dangers of the life class?

First: the growth of an attitude that the studio is not merely a very narrow segment of life, but that as far as art is concerned it is life. The development of a conditioned reflex: 'What I do in the life-class, very important people appear to regard as art, therefore it is art, therefore by continuing to work as though I were still in the life-class I shall make art.' The evidence that this is a widespread attitude can be seen in every exhibition.

Second: that the approach to study becomes the approach to art. Detachment, a desire to be objective, a belief that vital art can be a matter solely of passionless self-subjugating discipline. Remember that the substance of art is emotion, emotion taking on material form.

That in receiving from your tutors and your fellow students various technical tricks you may come to believe that these are art itself. Guard against becoming a conjurer's apprentice, acquiring a set of tricks which you can pass off as art and which you can, at some future date, teach to others in the same way. Beware of the dynamics of the life-class establishment, which can be inherited not only from tutors but from students of long-past decades.

60

Guard against the received image of a study, the clichés such as the double-head trick or the hand that moved. Worship neither completeness nor incompleteness, and above all do not allow yourself to visualize your final result, for to do so will inhibit your powers of discovery.

You must anyway face the fact that much of your early years will be involved in doing battle with received images. Burlington House and the Venice *Biennale* are typical academies of the received image, and I believe your greatest protection against these is your struggle with objective reality. But you must cultivate a degree of intellectual honesty which is by no means common, so that when you say to yourself, 'I am engaged in study' you do not allow yourself to think of the diploma it may get you, or the possible red spot. Do not allow your fear of being thought insensitive to seduce you into thoughts about ways of making your work look attractive. Do not be preoccupied with style, study for yourself, for no one else, and for nothing else, and treat the activity seriously or leave it alone. Above all do not do one thing and pretend to yourself that you are doing another.

With luck you will discover that wherever your intention is primarily objective, the tutor, if he is a good one, will be able to help you a great deal. You should seek his aid in these pursuits, just as you should fly from him as from poison ivy in other circumstances. But when he teaches you to put up an armature, or to square up a painting, or shows you how a man may draw as though his eye were a camera lens, and his optic nerve the only inlet to his brain, make sure that you are very much on your guard. Take care that when he opens your eyes to what he may call objective reality, he is not just opening them to his reality.

The wish to justify and explain is such a strong human desire that we, the tutors, are frequently caught unawares. Too often as we go about our business of illustrating techniques or acting as a second pair of eyes we unwittingly behave as if teaching art were possible. I know that when we are caught out in this abominable act, we usually about face immediately and proclaim louder than anyone else that of course art cannot be taught. But the damage is sometimes almost beyond repair. A verbal critique delivered as though sanctioned by objective truth itself, has stuck, and the student will only rid himself of this incubus with much pain and perhaps not until many years later.

You must beware of the wiles of those of us who would be gods to you, who, being but human, are inflated by adulation from those who seek our patron-age, we who become gentle egomaniacs, dispensers of gnomic statements, and handers out of the fruits of position. A word in the right ear, and a teaching job grows into your hands. A committee coaxed, and a coveted scholarship materializes. Because of the flattery we receive we begin to think we know; perhaps very little, but even that minute particle can become a millstone round someone's neck. Be passionately sceptical over all things which you are taught.

You need not fear that your results will ever be as objective as your intentions; quite the contrary. Art is not always made by consciously trying, although I do believe that being aware of a desire to create, to mani/ fest newness, is not the despicable thing some art/haters would have us believe.

I said at the beginning that study was a matter of intention rather than product, but I want to consider for a moment what may sometimes result. Even today I believe there can be great and moving works which originate from the intention of study. They will, how/ ever, be unfashionable, because they will not conform to the present received image of progressive contem/ porary art, and disappointingly, many people of great sensibility will appear to get no pleasure from them.

But the act of study, pure and uninhibited, raised to a sublime level by strength of intention, can become a Promethean battle with the objectivity of things, and the consequence, be it drawing, painting, or sculpture, can express this. A good study can be as much a work of art as anything else made today, although its message may be an unfamiliar one to many. Sometimes you will find yourself in the wrong company. Sometimes you will receive approval from those whose views you despise, but that is a hazard you must endure; there are worse fates.

Unfortunately today the life/class, where it exists in

more than name, has largely fallen into disrepute except among the squares of the art world. The commonest experiences are the class which merely pays lip service to the idea, and the academy where the ossified disciplines of the nineteenth century are still rigidly enforced.

There are many art schools where vast numbers of works proclaim their author's loathing of the human animal. These objects so offend and terrify me, that there are times when I feel it would be better to do away with art schools entirely, but in my more optimistic moments I realize that this is not an inevitable situation. There are many things which may be done; some of the steps needed are practical and involve the expenditure of money, others depend on a change of heart on the part of those responsible.

Among the practical steps I would suggest (1) much greater efforts to entice better, by which I mean more beautiful, more vital, more virile, models; (2) reduction in the size of life-classes and improvement in the planning and design of their premises. Far too many life-rooms are dreary, north-lit factories, reminiscent of the cellars beneath public museums. They involve a positive effort on the part of the student, if he is to remain optimistic and cheerful in their gloomy and seedy atmosphere. In general everyone must fight to destroy the conventional dynamics of past generations of students and tutors, the false gods set up by ossified tradition, to whom far too many life-classes are dedicated. Over the past 150 years the life-class has become too often the temple of system worship, of creative accidents which in their origins were vital and rewarding, but which in the course of time have become ends in themselves. False gods such as the science of measurement, the worship of imitation, and a horde of insane routines dedicated to so-called objectivity have accumulated and must be thrown out.

In my view of the needs for creative development, the life-class should have an honoured place, but it should either be dedicated to the intention of study or disbanded. This does not mean that I do not appreciate that a student will often want to work creatively with reality before him. But let us not call this a life-class, and let tutors keep out except when invited.

About 'the few words' they are asked to say under these circumstances I shall have something to contribute in my last lecture. Meanwhile you might like to give thought yourselves to the question of what, if anything, may profitably be said about a painting or a sculpture as a work of art: what meaning if any can be attached to the noises of approval or disapproval one man may make about another's creative efforts.

Before I finish, I want to say something about drawing in connection with the life-class, and what I have to say is particularly directed to sculpture students. It concerns the dangers of imitative techniques which so easily become part of a sculpture student's stock-in-trade, and is also related to the different ways sculptors and painters tend to respond to experience.

Put over-simply, the difference is that between seeing and knowing.

Now, the act of perceiving for the general run of painter students is largely a visual one. This is particu-larly noticeable if you contrast the general atmosphere of most painting studios with that of sculpture rooms. In the painting studios the students are static, there is very little movement, each man has his place and there is the model. In the sculpture studio, a continual to-ing and fro-ing takes place between the student's place of work and the model. His work is not a pure response to visual experience from a single viewpoint, he is build-ing with what he learns in other ways as well as from what he sees, and sculpture is quite rightly regarded as much more than the results of optical experience. In a quasi-objective sense this is often said to give the sculptor certain advantages, but I think there are also dangers. For art is artificial, and there is often in sculp-ture study a danger of the student's losing sight of this fact. In this connection drawing is most valuable. It is furthest from my thoughts, of course, to suggest that drawing should be regarded solely as a means to an end, for drawing is a great art in its own right, but technically, drawing involves only a sheet of white paper and a pencil, and the result is physically two-dimensional. This means that the student is involved in the translation of a three-dimensional experience into a two-dimensional conception—an activity in which dimensional imitation plays no part.

Too often I see sculpture students working in a way

which can only be described as that of imitating life full size, a valuable enough exercise on occasion, but, exclusively pursued, completely sterilizing. There is my model, here is my lump of clay; what am I doing? I am making *this* like *that*.

A student can often go on doing this sort of thing for a very long time, fending off criticism, effectively preventing anyone around being very helpful. Under these circumstances it is often difficult for anyone, including the student himself, to assess his progress or even his potential ability. But put a sheet of drawing paper in front of him, and instead of trick modelling full-size he is forced to think, and being forced to think he will, with luck, discover the limitations of thought and be driven, consciously or unconsciously, towards the exploitation of such sensibility as he may possess.

It should not be necessary to have to say this, but it seems to me that sculpture students are quite often prone to forget that, like painters and poets, they are supposed to be artists.

Five: The Creative Island

IN my serial-planned art-school after a period of intensive study of history, technology, and traditional skills,
the student, although still under the school's aegis, is
found private studio space. From then on, for good or
ill, he directs his own development. He is given all the
technical facilities he wants, is free to make contact
with tutors and share the life of the establishment if he
wishes. The finance needed to make all this possible is
provided by drastically cutting the number of students
given full-time education.

I believe that throughout the initial period he will be
encouraged by the thought of the supported freedom
which will ultimately be his as a matter of right instead
of a chancy possibility depending on patrons outside
the school or his public relations with tutors. For it
seems to me that the most crucial period in a student's
life is the two or three years after leaving the relative
security of the school in which he has worked. Not
enough responsibility has been accepted for this
situation. For a period of four or five years the average
art student in this country is financially supported, and

surrounded by people dedicated to his welfare, and during this time he develops an awareness, one hopes, of the ruthless standards and integrity which he must display if he is going to achieve anything in his vocation. But in contra-distinction to architectural students and others, he will acquire little if anything which will enable him to earn his living at the work he has chosen, and suddenly the course is over and the support withdrawn.

I do not think that my demand for a period of sup-ported freedom is sentimental. For one thing it is based on the belief that for an artist to get outside support he must show that he deserves it, and that the pattern of art education as arranged at present is such that it is not only difficult to find the right students for scholarships, but having found them to provide them with the facilities they require to begin their real work. Creativity in painting and sculpture is not a group activity; it requires many kinds of freedom—physical, intellectual, and moral—freedom from the temptation to concern oneself with anything other than discovering the nature of one's talent. I would like as many students as possible to face the full and quite horrible responsibility of working with no other purpose than to express them-selves creatively, and with no excuse for failure beyond their lack of talent and application.

These facilities being given on the basis of what I call the 'no-excuse principle', the student would work, if he did work, for the reason that he had no reason not to, and his work would be the reward of his in-built sense of guilt at not being creatively active.

As things stand at the moment society gives too many students too many excuses for failure. A man should recognize the reasons for his failure; he should be given enough freedom to recognize—if it is the case —that he does not really want to make art at all. This is an almost impossible situation to appreciate if a student is working under circumstances which allow an easy transfer of his allegiance from art to diploma-getting and artmanship generally. Under a system adopting the no excuse principle, the student would not be able to feel how much better his work would be if only he had:

a studio, private, personal and well equipped;

enough materials to let himself go;

no worries about how to keep himself and perhaps a wife and family;

no need to be tactful with tutors or patrons to whom he owed his facilities.

As there would be nothing standing between him and his guilt if he found himself unproductive, there would be no scapegoat to absorb responsibility. He would be having his chance, he would know it, and know that everyone else knew it too. No longer being able to concentrate on being a good student according to the rules of the establishment, he would develop full self-awareness as a necessity, and he would find out how strong his drives really were.

This situation does in fact work in the way I suggest;

I have some evidence. I was myself a sculpture Fellow at Leeds, which was a creative island made possible by Peter Gregory's insight. I have some personal knowledge of the way people here in England react to scholarships and grants generally, and I have information about the way the 'resident genius' scheme works in the United States.

Now to consider in more detail the kind of problems which will force themselves on the student's notice.

But don't misunderstand me; I attach no moral imperatives to my suggestions. The creative island idea is that the student should feel severed from establishment imperatives. Of course he will not be free from pressures—but they will be wider in origin and approximate more closely to what he will experience later on outside the school.

He must always be on guard against his idea of art being replaced by an idea of freedom or morality or something else. He will be his own master, and consequently the hardest master he should ever experience. He will be free to follow his own nose and perhaps discover that he hates the idea of where it leads him. He will, during this time perhaps, have his first opportunity to see himself as an artist, and may come to the conclusion that he does not like the look of himself in that capacity. Recognizing that all great artists in the past have been prolific, he may discover that for the previous four years he has been following a false trail, and that the last thing he really wants to do is to make a lot of paintings or sculptures. He will discover the dangers of free speech—the fact that any man has only a certain measure of creative vitality, and that if he uses it up in one form of expression it is not at his disposal for another.

Being able to work in privacy, he will be able to give less self-conscious attention to the creative accidents with which he comes in contact. He will be able to do things which he suspects may be foolish, but which, in point of fact, may lead to his greatest discoveries—he will be able to do this because of his privacy. He will be able, for instance, to begin work on a reclining woman, and in turning it upside down to insert an armature discover that he is landed with an object which might well be the beginnings of a standing man; and because he has no one at his elbow he may feel free to give it a run for its money without loss of face. As well as the big creative accidents he will be alert to many smaller ones. The strange things which happen when, after working in plaster for two years, he suddenly begins to work in wax, the way the material he uses and the means adopted nudge and push him in directions which seem of their own volition.

At this stage the student will feel the need to become his own critic, for the discovery that one both makes and judges is a necessary one in the life of any artist, but a difficult one to make when immersed in the hierarchy of an art school. Here the true relationship between thinking and making may well become apparent for the first time.

I have often myself recognized the fact that however

exciting the ideas appear to be which I take to the studio in the morning, if I have not forgotten about them within half-an-hour, then that working day is a bad one. One of the first things one learns about being a working artist as opposed to a theoretician, is that the work comes from a level far below the top of one's head, and that, for all one knows, one's life is largely determined by the seemingly spontaneous behaviour of one's hands.

During this period of creative freedom the student will have to be as much on guard against substitutes for aesthetic values as at any time in his life. Determined to preserve his desire to make things right, to make them smell right or look right or feel right, to avoid bolstering himself up as a moral person, or disguising from himself that he really hates art.

The physical shape of a creative island needs little description; obviously it consists of an adequate but not grand studio, enough money to keep the student in near poverty and his dependents at something above that level, technical facilities on a generous scale, and people with whom to discuss his problems when he feels the need, and a general overall sense that he is on his own and is himself the best and only reliable judge of his own efforts. He will be free to experience the deepest of depressions, the strongest conviction that he is wasting his life, and like Giacometti that the one thing he lacks is 'talent'. He will discover, as we all

73

discover, that no achievement in the past will assuage his present misery. There will be no release, he will have to go through with it. He will, during these miserable times, often have to concentrate on developing enough energy merely to put one foot in front of the other, not even in the hope that things will get better later on. But he will discover for himself various ways of coping with this situation.

I have found, for instance, that there are great benefits in working on a number of projects at the same time, a device if you like for spreading one's commitments. Thus, having worked oneself to a standstill on, say, a seven-foot piece of sculpture, it is just possible that instead of going out and shooting oneself, one may suddenly realize that another object in the studio, small perhaps, or directed towards an entirely different problem, may commend itself enough to demand attention; and immediately this happens the situation breaks. Similarly by having a large number of things going at the same time there are usually, during the bad periods, harmless technical things which require to be done, such as making bases, moulds, and so on.

I am not sure whether painters have available to them the same devices, but I imagine that to some extent there must be equivalents. A trick, if you like, that I have found most useful in really bad times, when on looking round everything seems hopeless and worthless and there seems to be but little point in doing anything at all, is to get a large bowl, half-fill it with water and top it up with plaster. Immediately I am driven by my natural meanness to find a use for that mixed plaster, before it becomes waste. That pound of plaster used in desperation has very frequently triggered off a whole sequence of activities which have been enough to get me out of the doldrums. For sculpture, like life generally, is very much a matter of one thing following another.

Separating himself deliberately from establishment values, the student, as I have said, must begin to be his own critic, and at this point I want to make a few comments about the aesthetic problem.

Consider a few traditional aesthetic questions, such as: What is the nature of the goodness or badness we attribute to a picture? In a general sense, with what is it connected? From what aspect of human affairs can we say, with some point, herein is the source of aesthetic pleasure?

Should we look upon paintings as some kind of 'solid noise' made by painters releasing their emotional response to experience and little else, or communication objectively accepted as being about artists' experiences? Or should we look at and judge an art-object simply as we do an object in the rest of nature, and concern ourselves entirely with examining its capacity to stimulate responses in observers without reference to its origin? It is quite evident that any comprehensive view of art must involve us in trying to do each of these things. But this still leaves the question of what characterizes the work itself as an object, and the question of the objective existence of its qualities, if it can be said to have any. You see, before one can really begin to think about aesthetics seriously, one is involved in primary philosophical questions: questions of meaning and perception and objectivity of being and existing and knowing and feeling and so on. Or consider practical or tutorial or critical questions such as, How useful to society or an individual is it for a critic to say this is a good picture? How helpful or unhelpful or damned meaningless is it for a tutor to say: You have got this right or you have got this wrong? All these questions lead backwards and forwards, they are general philosophical problems, and in my view no attempt so far to produce a unified field theory of aesthetics has been at all successful. Imagine for a moment an equilateral triangle; men standing on each side ask separate questions. One says: What do we mean when we say this is beautiful? Another: To what extent can we claim that a picture has objective qualities? The third: Can the qualities of pictures be described by us so as to be recognized by others as being the same? If there were a unified answer to the aesthetic problem, then it would be inside the triangle, and functionally related to the base-line questions which we ask, but in contrast to classical philosophy (which sought to produce a unified answer to all human questioning) we no longer, I think, hope for a comprehensive answer.

More than this, I believe that nowadays we suspect that this comprehensive total-pattern-making-desire is in fact something which derives from our own need to organize sensation in order to make use of it. Comprehensive answers may be simply a projection of our own structural acceptance mechanism. Anyway I suggest that unless our art form is philosophy, we confine ourselves to asking practically useful questions, without worrying too much about their interrelationship or their universal validity.

Here, as an indication of the sort of thing I have in mind, are a few 'answers', but please remember the context in which I offer them:

(1) In art as in morality is *good* best qualified by *for whom*? Yes. Think, not so much of art objects having qualities, as of art-object-percipient relationships having qualities. For instance think of the social-realist-Berger relationship or the Sylvester-Giacometti relationship or the Alloway-de Kooning relationship.

(2) The most objective statement we can make about good art is that art which is found to be good for a large number of people over a long period of time may usefully be called good. In other words: Good art lasts, and what lasts is good. In practice this is not so evasive or unhelpful as perhaps it sounds.

(3) Good relationships between a picture and a percipient probably relate in various degrees to all the following:

a. The observer's response to directly recognizable associative signs. (I like pictures with girls and yellow jugs, or I like girls and no jugs or jugs and no girls.)

b. The observer's response to symbols which are not directly recognizable discursively. (Not verbaliz-able, either because we only accept their significance at a sub-conscious level, or because they exist at a subliminal intensity only, or that they merely defeat verbal analysis for some other reasons.)

c. The observer's response to form and shape at a primarily physiological level (please note that I do not support separating 'physical' from 'mental' except in a very general way for practical purposes). By this sort of response I mean empathy: responding physically to an uplift form or a landscape form; projecting oneself empathetically into the forms of the work.

d. Responses due to the existence and effects of pattern acceptance arrangements in our cerebral structure.

(4) The noises we make about objects put before us may well be worth no more than their comfort value: e.g. the noises a painter makes to go with his work, because he feels he is protecting himself against critical attack when he makes them: verbal justifications of abstraction or realism or fragments or whatever. Some artists have to preach that nothing can be said which is of value, equally, others have to hand out a complete verbal work of art to go with their paintings or sculptures. Similarly we must allow for the noises a critic may make to show what side he is on, or a tutor

78

to assure himself that he is earning his pay. But this does not mean that we never get a sensation that someone has said something most appropriate about a work. Obviously there are severe limitations to the verbal analysis of non-discursive symbols, but because of this it does not mean that no verbal works intended to describe or explain are of practical value.

A critic's writing does not have to be literally informative—it would certainly be a poor outlook for them if this were so. For one thing, it can be appreciative in a personal subjective sense, and not less valuable because of this, for a line of prose does not have to be scientifically informative in order to leave the reader with a sense of having experienced some kind of enlightenment. Do not forget, one cannot analyse a line of good poetry so that nothing escapes our conscious examination.

(5) While in an elementary sense there are no absolute canons, nevertheless there are canons of a sort, and they probably correspond to the biologically and culturally advantageous elements of human evolution. Thus there are human-western-European canons, human-oriental canons, and for all I know dog-Patagonian canons. I think they must correspond to normal evolutionary values, for example youth–smoothness, age–wrinkledness, curve–vitality, death–concavity, and so on. I regard these canons as long-term values operative as much in upper paleolithic times as now. But their over-intensification and perversion variants should, in my opinion, be thought of as

79

taste canons, perhaps cultural evolutionary values which
do not vitally correspond to biological-evolutionary
ones. I am sure the 'what is good taste' questions are
answerable in these terms. In short, when we say we
appreciate it means we are responding to biologically
connected expressiveness and culturally determined
values, and that these latter are engendered by learning
the rules, or just by being exposed and thereby developing conditioned responses.

However long or short your period of supported
freedom, ultimately you will be living in the same
world as the bourgeois business man—the Mr Zero's
and the moralizers. You will be involved in preserving
your values against theirs. You will be in the world of
the art critic and the weekly art journalist, and you will
recognize them as men with a point of view deserving,
if not approval, at least consideration. With regard to
the bourgeoisie I have nothing to say except to remind
you that they are also human. But with regard to the
critics I think perhaps there may be something that can
usefully be said.

Remember always that their evaluations are those of
men and not of gods. Their responses are subjective
and human and fallible, and they have their way to
make in the world even as you have. Sometimes your
work will be a staircase for them, at others an obstacle
which they will try to demolish, but what is important
is what happens in the long run.

There is only one way to deal with the critic, and
that is to try to get him into perspective. I suggest that

you concern yourself quite a bit with art criticism—that is to say read it regularly, and endeavour to discover the standpoint from which the critic delivers his judgments; to recognize the human being that stands in the shadow behind the printed word which looks so authoritative. From this you will come to know what Mr X is after and what upsets Mr Y. It will avoid your being over-despondent when you are attacked, and equally, I hope, prevent you from being over-pleased when you are praised. You will come to recognize that a critic has at his disposal a wide variety of sticks with which to beat the artist whose work he despises or fails to understand. What one man may call sensitive another may describe as weak, and what to Mr X is strength and power, to Mr Y is coarseness and vulgarity.

We all agree on the qualities we would like to find in art: sensibility, emotional conviction, technical skill (at one and the same time complete and yet unobtrusive), a power of organization, and a built-in mechanism to tell us how to approach it. There are not, even in the figurative-realist arguments, great discrepancies in what is demanded; the differences occur in the assessment of how much of this and how much of that.

But if for one reason or another you feel you cannot involve yourself in reading criticism, then it is better to leave it alone entirely. The one thing I advise you *not* to do is to limit your reading of the critics to those occasions when they are discussing you, because if you do, not only will you give excessive importance to their statements, but you will in fact have no mechanism whereby to judge their origin. To be praised by a critic whom you despise is a miserable experience, worse in my view than being despised by a critic you admire.

If you feel that I have wasted your time by discussing a policy for creative development which is of little use to you at school under present circumstances, I am sorry, but I hope you will not look at it like that. I believe by organizing your work somewhat as I have indicated you could, even within the existing frame/work, put into practice much that I have suggested.

Make your initial contacts with history and tech/nology as intense and searching as you can, treat the question of study as seriously as you can, and make your later time at school or when supported by a studentship as detached from received objectives as possible.

Thank you for listening to me so patiently during these hot summer afternoons. I particularly want to thank Patric Proctor for enduring a very long tape recording of some of the initial ideas, and the members of the staff who have been so generous as to listen to my views and make their most valuable contributions.